Original title:
The Watcher's Time

Copyright © 2025 Creative Arts Management OÜ
All rights reserved.

Author: Kieran Blackwood
ISBN HARDBACK: 978-1-80586-082-2
ISBN PAPERBACK: 978-1-80586-554-4

A Tapestry of Seconds

In a world where clocks just laugh,
Ticking jokes and silly gaffes.
Each minute wears a vibrant hue,
Dancing seconds, a waltz anew.

The hour hand can't keep the beat,
While coffee cups just loom and greet.
With every sip, time takes a spin,
As morning laughs and night slips in.

A Roomful of Echoes

Whispers bouncing off the walls,
In a hall where silence calls.
Every tick brings humor near,
Where laughter's clock is crystal clear.

A chuckle drags the minutes long,
While seconds skip in bright-eyed throng.
Time's antics spin the air so light,
As echoes giggle through the night.

Time's Fidelity

Tick-tock, the jesters twirl,
Racing skirts in a playful whirl.
Each second twinkles with a grin,
As time plays hide and seeks within.

In this dance, no foot's misplaced,
Just laughter filling every space.
With each heartbeat, humor climbs,
A melody wrapped in silly rhymes.

Paradoxes in the Dusk

Questions hang on twilight's lips,
Do shadows dance? Or take their trips?
As moments fumble, time slips by,
With a wink, it waves goodbye.

In the dusk, the jokes collide,
With silly thoughts that laugh and glide.
Ticking clocks in silly tune,
Make every second feel like noon.

A Gaze Beyond the Veil

Peeking through a curtain,
Where all the clocks just freeze,
A cat gives me a wink,
And dances with the breeze.

Tickles on my earlobe,
As seconds take a nap,
The goldfish starts a meeting,
To plan their next big flap.

Balloons float by my window,
In colors bold and bright,
They remind me of my dreams,
Taking off in sheer delight.

So I laugh at shadows,
That linger in the room,
They play hide and seek with me,
In a cartwheel of perfume.

The Unheard Sound of Time

In the attic, whispers fly,
A squirrel finds a clock,
It pulls it, legs a-swinging,
Like a kooky parrot rock.

Cornflakes rain in slow-mo,
As breakfast looks away,
I bet it knows the secret,
Of how ducks learn to play.

A turtle holds a party,
With donuts on a plate,
The candles are all wobbly,
But geese, they celebrate.

Behind the clock's bright face,
I spy a jolly face,
He grins, and starts to giggle,
As time becomes a race.

The Sentry's Lament

Up on the tower, I sit all day,
My snacks are scattered, they'd better not stray.
A pigeon lands near, it takes my last fry,
I shout at the skies, 'Oh, how time can fly!'

With heavy eyelids, I nod and I sway,
I'll nap for a moment, or maybe an hour,
But with my good luck, I'll wake up in May,
To find I've been crowned with a flower.

Watching Hearts Beat

Up in the balcony, peering down low,
I see couples dancing, oh where do I go?
A wink in their eyes, a clumsy first step,
I chuckle and think, 'Is this love or a misstep?'

Tick tock goes the clock, as I sip my cold drink,
Their faces grow funny, I can hardly think.
A high-five gone wrong, that leads to a fall,
I should win an award, for watching it all!

The Unfurling Hours

Round and round goes the merry-go-round,
As I keep my eyes wide, what joy can be found?
The minutes are giggling, the seconds play tricks,
While I count the moments, they're mixing up clicks.

Time spills like lemonade, sweet and quite tart,
I juggle my duties, now that's quite an art!
With circus precision, I spin and I sway,
Each hour's a clown, in a playful ballet.

Beneath the Surface

In pools of mischief, I dive and I peek,
Laughter erupts, it's a giggly streak.
I watch as they splash, all the fun that they make,
Their serious faces just start to break.

Hidden in joy, like a fish with a grin,
I can hardly contain all the laughter within.
With bubbles of giggles, I gloat from my place,
While clocks tick away, I'm lost in this space.

Threads of the Unseen

In shadows where the sneaky socks roam,
   Tick-tock giggles echo in the dome.
  A clock that dances, not quite aligned,
    Silly secrets tangled in its mind.

With every tick, a prankster's delight,
Time wears a mustache, what a sight!
It pulls your leg when you look away,
   Whispering jokes in the light of day.

As Time Unfolds

The hands of fate do a jig and swirl,
As minutes flutter like a teasing girl.
Calendars laugh, they flip and slide,
While hours giggle, they cannot hide.

Daylight's a clown with a floppy nose,
Nighttime joins in, a jester that glows.
Time's a trickster, a playful sprite,
Turning mundane into pure delight.

The Eyes that Count

With clocks for eyes that wink and play,
Counting the seconds in a whimsical way.
They peer and poke at the snoozing sun,
Making sure that the fun's never done.

These playful orbs of the ticking fate,
Count each chuckle, never too late.
Time's a puppet, strings all askew,
Laughing at all the silly things we do.

Secrets of the Timeless

In the vault of hours, laughter's concealed,
Moments wink, their truths revealed.
A giggle slips through the hourglass' neck,
As silence trips, bound to misreck.

What lies behind the dial's facade?
Tickling tales of a time gone odd.
The riddle of clocks, a laughter spree,
Holding secrets, forever young and free.

Reflections on Forgotten Days

Mirror, mirror on the wall,
Your secrets make me giggle and fall.
Days unremembered, lost in a haze,
Yet here I am, trapped in this maze.

I spilled my coffee, missed the train,
Laughed at a cat dressed up like a saint.
Tick-tock, the clock begins to snort,
This everyday circus is quite the sport.

The Long Gaze

Peeping through the blinds with a sly little grin,
Wondering where the neighbors have been.
They trip on their shoes, what a glorious sight,
It's a sitcom out here, oh what a delight!

The garden's a jungle, the weeds have a dance,
I cheer for the bugs, they take their chance.
With popcorn in hand, I watch them collide,
Life through my window, a goofy joyride.

Chronicles of Stillness

In my chair, I sit like a stone,
Watching the dust bunnies claim their throne.
Pillows fluff up and giggle in glee,
As I contemplate lunch, but nap's calling me.

The clock strikes loud, yet time stands still,
A marathon runner? No, just a cat's thrill.
Chasing shadows, pursuing the light,
In this mundane moment, everything's right.

Warding the Hours

Brooms and mops in a tango so bright,
They dance on the floor in the soft, low light.
I stand with a grin, a war of my own,
To banish the dishes forever alone.

Tickle the clocks, make them laugh out loud,
Time can't control me, I'm too damn proud.
With cupcakes and laughter, I'll take on the day,
Here's to the mayhem, hip-hip-hooray!

Mementos of Awareness

In the attic, dust bunnies play,
Giggling at things left for the day.
Old clocks tick-tock, a funny sound,
Marking moments lost and found.

A sock puppet gives me a wink,
Says he knows more than I think.
Life flew by on a roller skate,
While I was busy calculating fate.

Slivers of Eternity

I chased my shadow down the lane,
It tripped me up, what a pain!
But laughter burst like bubbles pop,
Eternal giggles, non-stop.

A cat with glasses reads the news,
While I'm still wearing mismatched shoes.
In this living archive of grins,
We're all just waiting for life to begin.

The Echoing Silence

In echoes loud of silent screams,
Socks lose battles, or so it seems.
The ghost of pizza haunts my night,
While I debate if it's wrong or right.

A rubber chicken on my shelf,
Says, 'Laugh a little, be yourself!'
Time slips away, with a wink and nod,
Turns out my laughter's a gift from God.

A Dance with Shadows

My shadow tangoed with the light,
Stepping on toes, what a sight!
It whispered puns, absurd and bold,
In the spotlight, I felt old.

With every twirl, I burst with glee,
As my slippers slipped away from me.
Playing hopscotch with the dark,
Who knew shadows could make their mark?

Time's Watchful Eye

Tick tock goes the clock,
I jest with every tock.
Time gives me a wink,
As I stop not to think.

Calendar pages fly,
Like birds in the sky.
Each day a surprise,
With chocolates and pies.

I snooze while it darts,
Like a kid with new arts.
Time's playing a game,
And I'm not to blame!

And every new hour,
I've grown quite the flower.
In laughter, I find,
The joy of mankind.

Secret Seasons

Spring shows up in socks,
While winter still blocks.
Timelines jumbled around,
Like lost puppies found.

Summer wears shades bright,
While autumn takes flight.
The seasons collide,
In a comical ride.

I dance with the breeze,
In antics that tease.
Leaves play hide and seek,
As laughter hits peak.

Time spills out like sand,
In a fidgety hand.
I chuckle in style,
As I stretch for a mile.

Dance of the Timeless

Time breaks out in a jig,
Forgetting its big gig.
I twirl like a top,
While time says, "Don't stop!"

A waltz with the clock,
Makes me laugh, what a shock!
Seconds shimmy and sway,
In a silly ballet.

Ticking with glee,
As I spill my tea.
Time hops on one foot,
In a tuneful pursuit.

Each hour brings a cheer,
With a jiggle, not fear.
I dance with the light,
Till it's time for goodnight!

Eyelids of Dawn

Morning blinks bright-eyed,
While I barely slide.
The sun stretches wide,
In a silly pride.

Dawn teases my bed,
With dreams still unsaid.
I yawn like a bear,
While time pulls my hair.

Coffee spills like gold,
As the morning unfolds.
I sip and I sigh,
Through the chirps up high.

The day takes a dive,
In a hustle to thrive.
Yet I chuckle and grin,
At the mess I'm in!

Reflections in the Twilight

In the dusk we see them prance,
Tiny shadows start to dance.
A cat in socks, a dog in hat,
I wonder where they got the swag!

Under stars, things start to gleam,
Glowing eyes, or so it seems.
The neighbors don't know they're a show,
Dancing lawns, take it real slow!

A squirrel in shades, what a scene,
Nuts for snacks, a veggie queen.
They laugh and tease, and plot some more,
Who knew the yard was a dance floor?

Just a twilight's giggling glance,
Nature caught in a silly trance.
Whispers loud, they toast with glee,
To their antics, come and see!

The Watchful Eye's Voyage

Ahoy there, mate, with a twinkle bright,
Nibbling on chips, very light.
With a wink from above and a chuckle down low,
It's all about where the snacks tend to go!

Sail the seas of garden ground,
Where the oddest critters can be found.
Pirates of laughter, in broad daylight,
Frolicking pests, what a sight!

A bear with a tie, and a crab in shoes,
Tossing out insults, and playful blues.
Chasing seagulls, as they dive and swoop,
What a crew, and they form a loop!

A spoonful of joy, a splash of fun,
All creatures dance 'til the day is done.
In this voyage, oh so grand,
Laughter's where we all stand!

Shadows of the Past

Once a gnome, with a beard so fine,
Stood in shadows, sipping wine.
A garden party, a clever ruse,
Spilling secrets, breaking news!

Pumpkins gossip, with a squeaky voice,
Discussing how they made their choice.
To be the best on Halloween night,
They all burst out into delight!

A ghost on a swing, with flair and glee,
He tells of tales, as funny can be.
The past is winking, don't you agree,
With shadows dancing, wild and free!

Time's a jester, playing tricks,
In old gardens with crumbling bricks.
Whispers of laughter, echoes so bold,
In shadows where joy's retold!

A Chronicle of Observations

In the park, what do I see?
Pigeons plotting with wild glee.
A kid in a cape, a dog with flair,
They chase each other without a care!

Notes on benches, growing strange,
'Beware of squirrels,' they arrange.
Today they plotted an acorn raid,
While I just sat, utterly amazed!

Trees whisper stories, they know it best,
How every creature's a guest.
The fun unfolds in each leaf's rustle,
As time blends in jovial hustle.

High above, clouds drift and sway,
Observations dance, come seize the day!
In this chaos, how could I tire,
With hearts so light, and dreams on fire?

The Keeper's Gaze

In a tower so tall, with a view quite grand,
The keeper chuckles, with clock hands in hand.
He tickles the seconds, makes minutes run wild,
While jellybeans bounce, like a mischievous child.

With binoculars aimed at a squirrel so spry,
He wonders, "Is that critter late to comply?"
A laugh echoes softly from shadows so near,
As time takes a pause, just to steal a cheer.

A pendulum swings, making faces that grin,
Each tick marks a giggle, where laughter begins.
In this quirky realm, where moments are free,
The keeper's gaze dances in pure jubilee.

So if you catch sight of a clock full of glee,
Know that time can be silly, just wait and see!
For every tick-tock holds a joke or a jest,
In the keeper's gaze, life is simply the best!

Shadows of the Past

In the corners of memories, shadows do twirl,
They dance with the past, like an unruly whirl.
With a wink and a nod, they recall a good time,
Where laughter was currency, and antics, the rhyme.

Pictures flipped through, a goofy parade,
Of summer's mischief, and lemonade made.
A hat worn askew, and the dog on a leash,
With snapshots of laughter that will never cease.

Mistakes made in dress, like a plaid and polka mash,
Entwined with the moments, a colorful clash.
These ghosts of the old just want to bring cheer,
To remind us of fun, year after year.

So when you feel shadows creep into your mind,
Let them dance with the smiles that you leave behind.
For the past is a canvas, where joy thrives at last,
In the gallery of life, with shadows unsurpassed!

Echoes of the Unseen

In the halls of the unseen, echoes play tricks,
With whispers of laughter and light-hearted picks.
As time blows a kiss, and the clocks start to spin,
The echoes are grinning, inviting you in.

Behind every wall, there's a giggle or two,
Where shadows leap out, and the unexpected's true.
An echo of folly, like balloons in the breeze,
Defying the rules with the greatest of ease.

A door creaks open, revealing a jest,
Where the echoes conspire to put smiles to test.
With a jump and a hop, they skip all about,
Reminding us all what true laughter's about.

So catch the soft echoes that flutter and sway,
In moments of silence, they'll brighten your day.
For the unseen can sparkle, and playfully tease,
With echoes of joy that shall always appease!

Timeless Reflections

In puddles of laughter, reflections arise,
Where time takes a break, and nature complies.
A mirror to moments, where silliness reigns,
Glimpses of joy dancing, free from the chains.

"Is that my old self?" a smile sneaks out,
With socks of two colors, in fashion, no doubt.
The reflection just giggles, a cheeky old friend,
In timeless connections, where fun will not end.

As clocks pause and wink, giving sight to the soul,
Each laugh, like an echo, brings time to its goal.
For in every reflection, the jesters convene,
Transforming the mundane to something serene.

So look to the waters, where memories show,
A carnival mirror of laughter's sweet flow.
Because time, when reflected, shows what we find,
In the moments together, we're all intertwined!

Keeper of Shadows

In a corner, shadows dance,
With silliness they prance,
They giggle under the light,
Making a mess of the night.

A clock ticks with a cheeky twist,
It tells tales that can't be missed,
Every hour, a joke it spins,
While the stars just wear their grins.

The moon peeks through a dusty tree,
"Why are you so bright?" says he,
The sun winks, oh what a sight,
"Just trying to win this silly fight!"

So they bicker in the twilight hour,
Turning time into a chuckling power,
With shadows and laughter combined,
Time's nonsense, delightfully entwined.

Time's Endless Echo

Tick-tock goes the silly clock,
Echoes bounce with a friendly knock,
Every second shares a joke,
While the old walls laugh and poke.

The minutes wear silly hats,
Dancing with the playful cats,
"Catch me if you can!" they say,
While the hours just sway and play.

A playful wind whispers a tune,
Spinning tales under the moon,
Time's echo fills the air with cheer,
"Be quick now, the fun is near!"

Each tick is a giggle, a wink,
With every chime, we pause and think,
Is time a trickster, or a friend?
Let the laughter never end!

Eyes of Eternity

Peeking through a crystal sphere,
Eyes glimmer with a hearty cheer,
They spy on moments, big and small,
And chuckle at the rise and fall.

With a wink, they blink away the years,
Catching laughter, dodging fears,
"Time is silly," they seem to say,
"Join the giggles, come and play!"

A tickle from the sands of fate,
Races where the funny waits,
Sometimes lost, sometimes found,
With giggles that abound all around.

Like the sun that paints the sky,
With every hue, it waves goodbye,
And those eyes, oh, how they shine,
Crack a smile every time!

Chronicles of the Stillness

A book of time rests on the shelf,
Written by a playful elf,
Each page a tale of mischief bold,
In whispers sweet and stories told.

In stillness hides a teasing grin,
Moments dance, let the fun begin,
"Why hurry?" the pages plead,
"Watch the nonsense, that's the creed!"

Chronicles of laughter penned,
Where faces twist and giggles blend,
Not all stillness is calm and gray,
Sometimes it's a funny ballet.

So let the stories twirl and spin,
In every silence, let joy win,
For even in the quiet night,
Lies the heart of frolic and light.

Stillness in Motion

In a world where clocks do spin,
I danced with shadows, a goofy grin.
Tick-tock, the minutes play a game,
Yet here I am, still the same.

A squirrel raced by, I lost my place,
Chasing tails in a frantic chase.
The sun was high, the day was bright,
Should I nap? Nah, that's not quite right!

The flowers giggle as I trip and fall,
Time laughs too, it's having a ball.
Running in circles, what a sight to see,
I think the breeze just winked at me!

So here I stand, in motionless thrill,
With only laughter to fill my will.
A moment captured, in jest and cheer,
Time rolls on, yet I linger near.

The Keeper's Lament

I hold the sand that slips away,
Yet all I do is laugh and play.
Each grain a joke, so silly and light,
Who knew time could be such a fright?

As minutes vanish like puffs of smoke,
I try to catch them—oh what a joke!
Tick-tock, I fumble, I trip, I fall,
Keeping time should not be a brawl!

A chime resounds, and I raise my brow,
What's that? A reminder? Not here, not now!
Worries and woes? I'll push them away,
For laughter is king in this fleeting play.

So here I stand, with my hourglass tight,
Watching the merriment take flight.
Lament I might, with a smirk and a sigh,
Here's to the present—let memories fly!

Shadows at Dusk

The sun dips low, shadows prance,
I take a step, and we all dance.
They twist and twirl, so sly and spry,
I shout, they giggle; oh my, oh my!

A wobbly lamp adds to the fun,
Its flickering light shines on everyone.
Time slinks away like a cat so sly,
With purring laughter, it waves goodbye.

The trees whisper secrets in evening's glow,
As I chase my shadow, like a throw.
It trips and tumbles, leaps with glee,
What a whimsical sight—we're two, not three!

As dusk settles down, and stars take flight,
I giggle softly at the fading light.
For shadows at dusk, a lively parade,
In the dance of time, my heart is swayed.

Timekeeper's Soliloquy

Oh, the secrets I keep in this space of mine,
A tick and a tock, a joke divine.
As moments drift by, I wave with glee,
Who needs control when it's so carefree?

With every chime, I try and rhyme,
But silly me, I'm always late to prime.
Time fidgets and wiggles, a cheeky sprite,
I chase it around, what a playful sight!

I whisper to seconds, "Come back, my friends!"
Yet they just laugh as the giggle bends.
They tickle my thoughts with frolicsome grace,
In the realm of minutes, I find my place.

So here I stand, with laughter in mind,
A keeper of time, yet so entwined.
In this soliloquy, enjoy the flight,
For even the clock finds time to delight.

In the Quiet Between.

In corners dark, I sit and stare,
Watching socks that vanish in thin air.
The clock ticks loud, it's really a joke,
Time plays tricks, a mischievous bloke.

I see the cat, with stealthy pounce,
Chasing dust motes, in quite a bounce.
A squirrel laughs, he thinks it's all staged,
While I record how time's often outraged.

The kettle whistles, oh what a sound,
Spilling secrets that are quite profound.
But all my tea goes cold, oh dear,
It seems that boredom's the real frontiers.

In the quiet moments, joy takes flight,
While I juggle thoughts, a comic sight.
Caught in a loop, can't get it right,
It's funny how time just loves to invite.

Eternal Vigil

I sit in wait, with snacks galore,
For life's great show, always wanting more.
The sun's at noon, but so is my snack,
I laugh so loud, I'm missing the smack.

Clouds drift by, some look quite weird,
A donut here, a puppy appeared.
Who knew that time could stretch so much?
This popcorn bowl proves to be my crutch.

A car drives fast, it makes me frown,
Do they even know they're missing the crown?
The day rolls on, a jester's delight,
In this eternal vigil, I'm never polite.

With a wink and nod, I play my part,
This vigil's more of an art.
It's funny how seconds can twist and twine,
As I munch my snacks and sip on wine.

Eyes in the Shadows

In shadows deep, I catch a peek,
Of drummers marching, singing out of tweak.
A flock of ducks in a waddle parade,
They're looking fancy, but quite overplayed.

The clock strikes weird, what a show!
Dancing paperclips in a row.
A ball of yarn goes on a spree,
A feline ninja joins the jubilee.

With eyes wide shut, I watch the farce,
Why's the peanut butter flying like a star?
Days tick by with a giggle and snort,
Who knew time would hold such a court?

In these shadowy sights, joy takes wing,
From cookies that dance to cats that sing.
With laughter ringing, I cannot delay,
My shadows hold the best ballet!

Moments Between Moments

Between the ticks, I see them zoom,
The moments hover, like flowers in bloom.
A flick of joy, a dash of fun,
Why do they rush? Aren't we all one?

A chicken dance, in slippers bright,
Making time giggle with sheer delight.
I wave at clocks, they nod back slow,
So much to savor, why rush and go?

Spoons that clank and forks that twirl,
While life's a mess, we simply swirl.
Bubbles rise, and giggles burst,
In moments, life continues to thirst.

With silly smiles, we skip and glide,
Through moments fleeting, we take our ride.
It's funny how seconds ask us to stay,
In these moments between, come laugh and play!

The Unfolding Present

Tick-tock goes the clock,
With every second it does mock.
I dance with shadows, twist and sway,
As moments prance and slip away.

A sandwich right beside my phone,
It yells, 'Eat me!' all alone.
I'm lost in thoughts that roam afar,
Yet, here I am, beneath this jar.

The cat looks bored, the dog is wise,
Both keeping track of my sunrise.
Tickling time, it just can't wait,
What a silly, playful fate.

So grab a snack, let laughter ring,
As present wraps its goofy fling.
Each moment turns, a wild parade,
Oh, if only plans could be delayed!

Fragmented Seconds

Seconds split, like half a pie,
Why's the doughnut making me cry?
I count the crumbs that trail behind,
Time's tiny pranks, so unrefined.

The toaster pops, my toast takes flight,
Jam lands on pants, oh what a sight!
Tickling clocks and cereal spills,
Each breakfast brings its share of thrills.

In moments brief, we often fumble,
Chasing socks that like to tumble.
Time more like a game than a race,
Laughing as we drift in space.

With every minute that slips away,
Life's like a grand, ridiculous play.
So let's embrace this silly quest,
And laugh with joy, it's for the best!

Observing Tomorrow

Peeking through the curtains wide,
What's coming up? I'll take a ride.
Tomorrow's antics on the way,
Should I prepare? Nah, I'll just play.

I set my sights on sleepy dreams,
And wonder if they're bursting seams.
The future's like a bubble song,
Will I make plans or just tag along?

Chasing clouds with cotton candy,
Reality? It's really dandy.
Predicting laughs, we joke and tease,
Time's a breeze, just aim to please.

So bring on the shimmer, bring on the fun,
As we wait for tomorrow, let's quickly run.
With smiles and giggles along the line,
The future's bright, and it's all divine!

Threads of Continuity

Time weaves its threads in playful ways,
Tangled up in hilarious frays.
The yarn of life's a silly game,
Each twist and turn, never the same.

A knitted scarf that's far too long,
Worn backward, but it feels quite strong.
I trip on thoughts that soar and glide,
As laughter trips me up with pride.

Moments tug like playful strings,
Unraveling joy and all it brings.
In this tapestry, we find delight,
Dancing through day and into night.

So let the threads entwine and spin,
With every giggle, let's just begin.
For continuity flows like wine,
Pouring sweetness over life's design!

Eternal Vigil

On the wall, a clock that's sly,
Ticking loudly as I sigh.
A squirrel jumps, gives me a wink,
Time to laugh, or at least think.

Every second feels like years,
When a cat just stares and sneers.
Watching grass grow is no crime,
Just a case of timeless rhyme.

When the sun dips, off it goes,
Running late for who knows?
Dance with shadows in the night,
Also known as cat's delight.

Seconds of Silence

In a quiet room I sit,
Counting seconds, what a wit!
Nose itches, a sneeze is near,
What was that? It's just a deer!

Check the watch, it's not too late,
For a snack, or maybe fate.
I blink twice, the world goes still,
Sudden urge to climb a hill.

Time does laugh, it knows my plan,
As I try to outrun a pan.
Hold my breath, don't miss the cue,
But the pie needs a taste too!

Gaze on the Horizon

Staring far at nothing grand,
I'm the king of all this land.
Seagulls swoop, a wave takes flight,
Oceans smile as day meets night.

A sandwich flitters from my grip,
As if it's on a leisurely trip.
How can seconds tease so well?
In a moment, off they swell.

Waves pretend they're in a race,
And I'm just here, stuck in place.
An ant strolls by with such a flair,
Taunting me without a care.

Fleeting Moments

Time slips by like butter spread,
On a piece of toast, it's dread!
Every tick is but a tease,
Even clocks take time to sneeze.

Friends gather, stories bloom,
How did we end up in this room?
Laughter erupts, oh what a spree,
Who knew fun could set us free?

Chasing the moments that go quick,
A tap dance on the clock's thick stick.
Then I trip and spill my drink,
Oh, the joy of time to think!

The Timekeeper's Chronicle

Tick-tock goes the clock,
I overslept, what a shock!
Coffee spills, the cat runs,
Chasing time, not having fun.

Forgetful notes are everywhere,
My to-do list is quite a scare!
Each minute slips like buttered toast,
I swear I'm the time's cruelest host.

Juggling seconds, stumbling slow,
Where did that hour go, who knows?
With every tick, my plans collide,
In this race, I just can't hide.

As the sundial rolls its eyes,
I sneak past with my little lies.
Minutes laugh, and seconds cheer,
Oh dear me, it's almost here!

A Glimpse Beyond

Through the window, I peek out,
Time is playing, without a doubt.
Seconds dance on a silver line,
Like squirrels racing, oh so fine.

I grab my hat, it's half-past late,
But those hands move at a faster rate.
My watch is laughing, what a prank,
In this game, I'm but a crank.

I tried to plan for the whole week,
Yet here I am, still feeling weak.
Each hour winks with clever stealth,
Stealing joy, oh time, you elf!

With a quip and a cheeky smile,
I'm late again, but stay awhile.
These fleeting moments tick away,
But who needs time? Let's laugh and play!

The Observer's Retrospect

Beneath the ticking old antique,
I ponder all the tricks they seek.
How do they stretch and bend the day,
While here I am, just hit replay.

Photos fade, and calendars lie,
The month was April? Oh, my, oh my!
I lose the years like candy floss,
In this merry-go-round, what a loss!

I saw the hands do a little jig,
Should I dance too, or just a twig?
They point and spin, they've lost their grace,
Chasing tails in a dizzy race.

Friends say, 'Count your blessings, mate,'
But I've counted sheep, I'm still too late!
As every second rolls away,
I just grin and hum my way.

Fleeting Glances

The clock is winking, how absurd,
It told my dreams without a word.
A hiccup here, a stutter there,
How does it know to rattle my hair?

A flash, a dash, where did it go?
Just like my socks in the dryer's flow.
With every glance, I seem to miss,
That perfect punchline, what a hiss!

Daylight savings, oh what a jest,
An hour gained? I couldn't rest.
Time is like a stretchy band,
Just when I think I've got it planned!

So here I am, embracing fate,
With clumsy steps, I can't be late.
Let's laugh at seconds, dance with glee,
In the funny face of the 'not-me'!

Ceremonies of the Eternal

In a room full of chairs, folks come to sit,
They shout at the clocks, saying, "Don't lose it!"
A squirrel in a tux, takes notes by the door,
Whispers of nonsense, they keep asking for more.

The candles are dancing, the cake's on the floor,
A mime takes the stage, can you ask for more?
A jester in sneakers, wearing mismatched socks,
Recites all the fables, while juggling three clocks.

Laughter erupts like a sprinkled confetti,
As spaghetti flies past—a wild confetti!
With each silly ritual, the laughter grows loud,
Eternal celebrations, well done, this crowd!

So gather your marbles, toss wrinkles away,
In the circus of moments, come join the play!
Remember this folly as time ticks along,
For joy is the prize, and laughter's the song.

Watching the World Turn

Like donuts on wheels, the world spins and rolls,
Laughter and chaos, it's good for the souls!
A cat with a crown, leads a parade of fish,
While penguins on bikes grant each other a wish.

The sun wears sunglasses as dusk starts to creep,
And owls start their gossip while everyone sleeps.
A turtle with glasses checks off his to-do,
"Must practice my running; oh, what can I do?"

Each tick of the clock, brings a new silly dance,
While a frog in a top hat performs a great prance.
Squirrels hold meetings to plan for the night,
As stars fumble trying to twinkle just right.

The world spins in circles, oh what a delight,
With laughs as the currency, everything's bright!
Keep watching the glances, the giggles, the quirks,
For in this grand show, every moment just works.

The Burden of Memory

There once was an elephant, full of great tales,
Who forgot where he parked all his shiny new scales.
He searched through the bushes, called out to a bee,
"Hey friend, have you seen my most recent decree?"

A fish in a top hat just chuckled in glee,
"I saw them last summer, quite near the old tree!"
The elephant stumbled, tripped right over a stone,
"Memories are heavy, should I wheel them alone?"

A tortoise with glasses chimed in with a grin,
"Just write it all down, it's the best way to win!
And if things get wild, take a break and just snack,
It's hard to recall with a rumbling snack pack!"

So they gathered for dinner, the tales flowed like wine,
With burgers and laughter, their stories combined.
The burden was lighter with each passing bite,
And memories danced in the warm candlelight.

Eyes on the Horizon

There's a bird on a branch that thinks he's the dawn,
Sings songs of tomorrow, and breaks into yawn.
The world is so wobbly, he can't see below,
As clouds turn to pancakes and syrup flows slow.

A rabbit with flip-flops hops straight to the breeze,
Dreaming of jellybeans dangling from trees.
He squints at the skyline, where marshmallows bloom,
Whispering secrets that vanish too soon.

An octopus juggles the future and past,
While riding a bicycle, nothing's too fast!
With eyes on horizons, the journey's a blast,
As time keeps on ticking, but worries won't last.

So let's wave to the clouds, and dance with delight,
With laughter and whimsy, we'll soar through the night!
For wherever we look, whether near or afar,
Life's funny adventures will always be char.

Curator of Forgotten Moments

In the attic where odd socks dwell,
Memories giggle and tales compel.
Dusty hats with feathers ask,
What's your favorite silly task?

A rubber chicken has a grand parade,
While clocks chuckle in a time charade.
Dancing with old shoes, oh what a sight,
In this silly realm, everything feels right.

Lost in laughter, nobody follows,
Giggling echoes bounce like swallows.
Old trinkets whisper jokes untold,
As nostalgia turns a bit too bold.

So come join in this merry jest,
Where fun and folly are truly blessed.
The curator waves while laughter rings,
In a world of laughter, joy takes wings.

Echoes in the Stillness

In the hush, a whoopee cushion squeaks,
As silence dances, so absurd it tweaks.
Naps gone awry and hiccups galore,
Echoes of laughter behind each door.

A ghost with a tickle fights for a jest,
While shadows play cards, they laugh at the rest.
Boredom's just a balloon full of air,
Pop it and watch the fun snare.

Clock hands spin in a chaotic twirl,
As time trips over its own whirling swirl.
In stillness, the silliness unfolds,
Tales of daredevils and far-off scolds.

Laughter lingers in the quiet night,
Like fireflies dancing, oh what a sight.
In echoes and whispers, hilarity blooms,
Revealing joy in old dusty rooms.

The Seer's Perspective

Through spectacles thick, the visions collide,
A cat wearing socks goes out for a ride.
Future foretold in jumbles of fate,
With a grin, the seer laughs at the wait.

Frogs in tuxedos parade with glee,
While time winks slyly from under a tree.
Silly predictions draw curious folks,
Like pies in the face, or old dad jokes.

Visions of sandwiches dancing in line,
Pretend to be great, yet taste like old brine.
Crystal balls burst with puns on the side,
The seer finds wisdom in laughter's glide.

So raise a toast to the merry and mad,
In the tapestry of time, the fun's never sad.
For each moment holds a ticklish spree,
In the eyes of the seer, we all can be free.

Labyrinth of Time

In a maze made of clocks, we often stray,
Chasing our tails while the hours play.
Round every corner, a rubbery joke,
Squeezed from the past, provoking a poke.

Wanderers giggle at paths they explore,
Finding old sandals outside a door.
With laughter echoing through every bend,
Winding through nonsense, our favorite trend.

Lost in a riddle, we tumble and trip,
A banana peel leads to a slip.
Tick-tock confirms our fun little quest,
In this crazy labyrinth, joy feels the best.

So let's dance through this quirky charade,
Embracing the chaos each choice has made.
For in a labyrinth where smiles entwine,
Every twist and turn is destined to shine.

Subtle Shifts of Existence

A clock with a face that just won't smile,
Snoozes and winks, takes a break for a while.
Seconds slip by like socks on the floor,
While I ponder life's snacks, oh what a chore!

The hands play hide and seek with the sun,
Tickling each hour, oh isn't that fun?
While I chase shadows, they giggle and hide,
In the dance of existence, they take me for a ride!

Pancakes for breakfast, or was it just lunch?
Time's a great jester, and I'm in a crunch.
I swear just a moment, but now it's a day,
In this silly game, I'm just here to play!

A wink from the sandman, a chuckle from bed,
Why count all the hours when laughter is spread?
Life's subtle shifts are like jello on a plate,
Bouncing and wobbling, it just won't wait!

The Space Between

In the cozy gap where nothing is said,
Time wears its slippers, and dreams go to bed.
A giggle, a snort, what's that silly sound?
The clock's just a jester, and I'm still around!

Counting the seconds, like counting my toes,
Five little dancers in mismatched clothes.
The calendar's winking, oh what a sight,
Whispering secrets while I'm dimming the light.

Nimbus clouds float, with a giggle or two,
As moments drift by, they tickle my shoe.
The in-between laughs, like bubbles in tea,
Make every odd second feel carefree and free!

Life's little pauses, like hiccups in rhyme,
Are treasures discarded, yet fun every time.
So let's toast to the gaps, with a chuckle and cheer,
For in spaces between, we'll hold all that's dear!

Temporal Whispers

A whisper of minutes floats under my nose,
Like ticklish little fairies in pink fuzzy clothes.
They tease and they laugh, making shadows parade,
While I chase my thoughts like a high-stakes charade!

The minutes are mischief, with mischievous grins,
They tangle and jive, where the good humor spins.
A waltz through the hours with socks that don't match,
And clocks that play games like a sneaky old hatch.

Whispers grow louder with each passing hour,
A gentle reminder of laughter's sweet power.
So I join in the frolic, forget time for a bit,
In the whimsical world where I gladly submit!

The clocks all conspire, a party in sight,
As tick-tock and giggles unite in delight.
What a joyous recital, with sparks flying high,
I'll dance with their whispers, just me and the sky!

Episodes in Solitude

In the quiet abode, where silence wears shoes,
The minutes are knitting, thick yarns for my muse.
Time tickles the corners, wraps laughter around,
In episodes solo, where joy can be found!

My watch plays the fool, a clown with a grin,
Counting the moments like it's a game to win.
With coffee as sidekick, we plot and we dream,
In episodes of solitude, life bursts at the seam!

A dance of creation, where shadows can play,
Life's jumbled chapters, unravelling the day.
Tick-tock becomes music, a sweet little tune,
As I sip on the moments that sparkle like June!

In this merry affair, no rush, just pure fun,
With giggles and chuckles, each tick is well spun.
May the episodes linger, like a soft, warm glow,
In solitude's embrace, I'll relish the show!

Light and Shadow's Embrace

In the room a lightbulb flickers,
A shadow dances and then snickers.
The wall's a canvas full of fun,
As jokes appear and races run.

The couch a ship that sails through air,
While pillows laugh with carefree flair.
A shadow leaps, I give a chase,
But meet a chair, oh what a case!

Laughter echoes in this space,
As light draws chuckles on my face.
In every creak, a funny line,
As shadows twist, and stars combine.

The Fluctuating Pendulum

A pendulum swings left and right,
Like comedians in a playful fight.
Tick-tock antics all around,
In every motion, giggles found.

It teases time with silly dance,
Forgetting reason, skipping chance.
"Hey there clock, what's your game?"
It winks back, "Oh, just the same!"

The walls are cheering, join the fun,
As time unravels one by one.
A pendulum's jests, oh so sly,
Making seconds twirl and fly.

Timelines Intertwined

Moments tangled like spaghetti,
In crazy knots, all warm and petty.
Past and future have a laugh,
As they mix up the epitaph.

"What day is it?" one asks in glee,
"Your birthday, but it's next week, see!"
Time snickers, "What a lovely scheme,
Just dance around that twisted dream!"

Whirling memories, playful and bright,
Each tick a plot twist, pure delight.
As we spin through these jumbled lines,
We trip on giggles and clock designs.

Shadows Cast by Stars

Stars giggle high in the deep velvet sky,
Casting shadows that flutter and fly.
"Is that a cat or just a shadowy game?"
"Let's play tag with the moon, how lame!"

Below, the trees bend low with joy,
Their shadows twist, like a playful toy.
"Catch me if you can!" they tease the ground,
But laughter erupts, and joy abounds.

Stars fit snug in their twinkling home,
While shadows stretch out, like foam.
Together they giggle, twirl, and leap,
In a night that promises joy to keep.

The Timekeeper's Soliloquy

Tick-tock, the clock has a joke,
It laughs while we busy folks choke.
Time wears a hat, quite silly in form,
As seconds dance and rhythms swarm.

Minutes prance like a three-legged dog,
Whispering secrets under a fog.
Each hour, a puppeteer pulls the string,
Behind every laugh, a new spring.

Yet here I sit, in my dusty chair,
Counting the giggles, do I dare?
With each tick, my memory fades,
But the laughter, oh! It cascades.

So here's to time, a clown in disguise,
Winking at passersby with bright eyes.
Let's laugh with the jokes it tries to tell,
As we dance through this time, oh so well.

Unseen Connections

In the shadows, time's a comedian,
Bonding moments like a chameleon.
You can't see its tricks, but trust the show,
It's connecting the dots while we glow.

Mismatched socks, they wink at the clock,
Tickling the seconds, oh what a shock!
With every giggle, time spins its web,
Weaving laughter where secrets ebb.

You and I, we're tangled in fun,
Life's a race, yet we've barely begun.
Let's jump in puddles with mud on our shoes,
In the chaos of time, we'll never lose!

So here's a toast to laughter we share,
In the fleeting moments we brightly declare.
With each unwritten joke, let's stand tall,
For time's greatest comedy, we're part of it all!

Pages Worn by Time

Flip the pages, what do you see?
A history of blunders, just like me!
From upside-down hugs to slip-on shoes,
Time's a riot, nothing to lose.

Old tales of folly, they age like fine wine,
Secrets once silly, now all feel divine.
Dogs wearing glasses, and cats on the phone,
Each laugh captured, never alone.

So let's gather 'round, with tea and a tale,
The chronicles of clowns who bravely set sail.
Through ruffled pages of joy and regret,
Our laughs echo back, you haven't heard yet!

With every turn, more giggles abound,
In the library where lost smiles are found.
Time may wear down the cover, it's true,
But laughter stays fresh, forever anew.

Picturing the Unseen

In the gallery of time, a canvas appears,
Brushstrokes of laughter, allayed with cheers.
Moments picture framed, quite askew,
Artistry of mishaps, a view so true.

Doodles of joy hang high on the wall,
Each crack a story, every shadow a call.
Funky clocks spin in curious haste,
With splashes of color, not a moment to waste.

Laughter splatters like paint on the floor,
As we dance through corridors, yearning for more.
Unseen connections bloom wild and free,
With invisible threads linking you and me.

So grab a brush, let's create our own rhyme,
In this gallery where we chuckle with time.
For in this art, both silly and bright,
We're painting the unseen, with laughter in sight.

Ponderings of the Eternal

A cat on a ledge, so high and proud,
It scoffs at the clock, not bound by a shroud.
A tick and a tock, but it hears none,
For its thoughts on a nap have barely begun.

Time rolls like dough, squished by its paws,
What's a minute? Just a moment's faux pas.
An eternity passed in just one blink,
While humans debate, it's back to the sink.

In shadows it lounges, no care in its heart,
While clocks keep on ticking, it masters the art.
Eternal? Nah! A slice of a day,
It's here for the fish, and then it will play.

The Watchtowers of Memories

Up on a hill, the old towers stand,
With tales untold, they make silly plans.
One whispers secrets of socks gone awry,
The other just chuckles and lets out a sigh.

"Remember that time?" one tower would jest,
When they all flew high, like birds in their nest!
A pink elephant waltzed down the lane,
While a frog in a tux played a tune quite insane.

Through the clouds of memory, they watch and they grin,

Each giggle and guffaw rumbles deep within.
Time's just a trickster, with pranks left to share,
In the watchtowers of laughter, there's always fresh air.

Moments Held in Suspense

A kitten at play, about to pounce,
Time halts, everyone leans, the tension's announced.
Will it leap? Will it fall? What's next on the stage?
A moment stretched thin, like an overripe wage.

In the crowd, whispers, "It's going to fly!"
But the moment hangs low, like a well-timed lie.
Then, SPLAT! It dives into a pile of yarn,
And laughter erupts, "Oh, how you did charm!"

The audience rolls as confusion takes flight,
What's time if it pauses, then bursts with delight?
These moments hold laughter, they dance and they swell,
In the realm of the daft, they chronicle well.

A Seer's Chronicle

A seer with spectacles, forever astute,
Predicts with a grin, "Your breakfast? A fruit!"
But time plays its trick, and the toast starts to burn,
And all that he sees is a lesson to learn.

"Tomorrow, you'll trip, on a rogue little shoe,
Just heed my words, or it's all up to you!"
Yet slips in the kitchen make prophecies wait,
It's all in good fun, to laugh at our fate.

A crystal ball sparkles, pointing with glee,
"What's coming next? Could it be…a bee?"
With laughter resounding, the crowd rolls in mirth,
For the seer's great tales are of slapstick rebirth.

Gaze into the Abyss

In the depths of my chair, I really do stare,
Into the abyss, where socks go to fare.
There's a world of lost things, all wooly and blue,
I wonder if they're plotting, conspiring too.

Time tickles my brain, like a cat on a spree,
Chasing imaginary mice that never flee.
I chuckle and snort, as the clock takes a spin,
Counting all of my laughs, hoping I win.

An hour's just a blink, when you're stuck in a fight,
With a roll of the dice, and a game that feels light.
The minutes are jesters, they dance on the walls,
While I sip on my coffee and wait for their calls.

Oh, what a grand show, this chaos we pen,
With curtains of laughter, we do it again.
So here's to the moment, let's celebrate cheer,
For the giggles and wiggles are what brought us here.

The Guardian's Breath

A breathy old guardian, with a wink and a grin,
Sips tea from a kettle, while the day wears thin.
He juggles the ages, with clumsy delight,
Spilling drops of history, with a giggle by night.

Tick-tock goes the pendulum, a comical sound,
Laughter spills over, as chaos is found.
He tells silly stories, of clocks made of cheese,
And that time is a trickster that jumps like the breeze.

Each second has pom-poms, waving so free,
While hours do cartwheels, just to make me see.
In the carnival twilight, where moments collide,
The breath of the guardian fills every slide.

So I tip my hat, and join in the dance,
For in this odd folly, we all take a chance.
With giggles as currency, laughter the key,
The guardian's breath is where we all want to be.

Unraveling Time's Tapestry

In the loom of the ages, I find quite the mess,
Threads tangled in laughter, well, I must confess.
The fabric is funny, with patterns so wild,
I'm not quite sure why it looks like a child.

Each hour is a stitch, slipped in with a grin,
While moments unravel, and chaos begins.
Knots form in the way, of the big ball of yarn,
And here comes a cat, makes the whole thing a barn!

With clocks made of rubber and laughter for lace,
The tapestry giggles, in this whimsical space.
I wiggle and wobble through this colorful maze,
Chasing all of my giggles, like mischievous rays.

So let's weave together, a jester's delight,
Where time isn't serious and smiles are in sight.
For in this grand tapestry, woven so bright,
Laughter is timeless, our heart's pure delight.

Perpetual Observation

A wobbly old stool, where I sit with a laugh,
Observing the world, like a quirky giraffe.
I jot down the follies, of folks passing by,
Like the man with the hat that could soar in the sky.

Oh, time is a noodle, all wiggly and fun,
It sloshes and splashes, like water, it runs.
I can't help but chuckle, at clocks that run late,
Their tocks racing faster, for a twist of fate.

Each minute's a dancer, with two left feet,
Spinning in circles, but never discreet.
With giggles like confetti, they fly through the air,
I catch them with joy, and toss them with flair.

So let's toast to the moments, forever in play,
With laughter we gather, come what may.
In perpetual observation, we savor the rhyme,
For life's a grand circus, and it's always showtime!

www.ingramcontent.com/pod-product-compliance
Lightning Source LLC
Chambersburg PA
CBHW060140230426
43661CB00003B/505